Newfoundland Dog Traini

Dog Training for your Newfou

Expertengruppe Verlag

The contents of this book have been written with great care. However, we cannot guarantee the accuracy, comprehensiveness and topicality of the subject matter. The contents of the book represent the personal experiences and opinions of the author. No legal responsibility or liability will be accepted for damages caused by counter-productive practices or errors of the reader. There is also no guarantee of success. The author, therefore, does not accept responsibility for lack of success, using the methods described in this book.

All information contained herein is purely for information purposes. It does not represent a recommendation or application of the methods mentioned within. This book does not purport to be complete, nor can the topicality and accuracy of the book be guaranteed. This book in no way replaces the competent recommendations of, or care given by a dog school. The author and publisher do not take responsibility for inconvenience or damages caused by use of the information contained herein.

Newfoundland Dog Training

Dog Training for your Newfoundland puppy

EXPERTEN GRUPPE VERLAG

CONTENTS

ABOUT THE AUTHOR

Claudia Kaiser lives with her husband and dogs Danny (2 years old) and Daika (8 years old), in an old farmhouse in beautiful Rhineland, Germany.

At first only as a dog owner, but later and after 20 years actively training dogs, she has gained a lot of experience, helping other people to train their Newfoundlands. She formed the idea of writing this book in order to reach more people, than she could have in the local dog training schools and the small circle of dog owners to whom she gave personal coaching.

The publishing of this guide book is the fruit of considerable research, writing and editing. It is designed to be a guide for all budding Newfoundland owners, to help them get the difficult task of training right the first time, and to avoid those mistakes, which Claudia herself made at the beginning. She worked through her own bad experiences over the years, so that the reader does not have to.

Those who follow the tips and tricks covered in this guidebook are sure to have many years of pleasure from these unusual and wonderful companions.

PREFACE

Congratulations, you have made the excellent choice of welcoming a Newfoundland puppy into your life. You have also chosen to buy this guidebook. This way, you have already made two good decisions.

A puppy is a small bundle of energy. His clumsiness, fluffy fur and endless trust in you, his owner, will make everyone's hearts melt. This little Newfoundland will fulfil all your days and soon you will not be able to imagine life without him.

Before you read the next pages, you should know what to expect. This guidebook will not change your little treasure into a well-behaved dog overnight. The guide does not show you any shortcuts to success. Most importantly, reading this book alone will not change anything. Your success depends solely on you.

This guidebook will give you the necessary tools, not only to find your friend for life but also how to bring up a fear-free, happy and dependable Newfoundland. This book is based on a gentle method of training but it also requires adherence to strict rules and needs lots of patience. It will not always be easy to stick to the rules, particularly when you see his big, trusting dog eyes looking at you. But I guarantee, that it is worth it in the long run. Not only will you be rewarded for your work, but your Newfoundland will benefit even more.

Are you ready to invest a lot of time and love in your Newfoundland, not only during the first weeks, but also his whole life long?

Then you have made the right choice and you can read the following pages!

From my heart, I wish you both much success and good luck.

- Chapter 1 -

WHAT YOU NEED TO KNOW ABOUT YOUR NEWFOUNDLAND

The Newfoundland is a very special breed of dog, which is very different from many others. Training dogs involves many elements, which are the same for all breeds. However, every breed has its particular characteristics and traits which makes it unique. It is exactly these characteristics which are important in the training process.

If you want to get the best out of your Newfoundland training, it is important that you do not just give him a general training programme but one which is especially tailored for him. Some of these methods are much more important for your Newfoundland than, for example, a Chihuahua. It is these training modules that I will show you in the next few pages. But firstly, it is important that you get to know your dog's characteristics very well.

At an average height to the withers of 71 cm and a weight of 68 kg, the Newfoundland definitely belongs to the group of large dogs. It is not surprising to know that his fluffy fur gives him the nickname "bear dog". He gets his enormous power and stamina from his ancestors. As the name suggests, this breed originated on the Canadian Atlantic Island, Newfoundland. Although it is not exactly known how he evolved, it is believed that he comes from a mixture of those dogs which were brought to the island by European sailors and fishermen, and those dogs which were native of Newfoundland. In view of his thick undercoat, it is also assumed that some arctic Husky is part of the mixture. There was a theory that the Newfoundland was crossed with the big, black bear dogs of the Vikings, but this is not really considered plausible.

Irrespective of how he came to exist, his imposing stature, his weather resistance and his extreme love of water make him a favourite with fishermen and sailors alike. This dog was capable of pulling fishing nets or boats out of the water with unerring commitment. His tirelessness, despite appalling conditions, made him a popular working dog well outside the confines of

Newfoundland. He is often used as a lifeguard, due to his great love of water.

His character makes him less of a bear and more like a sheep. He is always relaxed, peaceful and very lovable. His loyal and good-natured eyes say all you need to know about his character, and despite his size, he is perfectly suited to family life. He loves children and develops strong relationships with them over the years. Due to his size, it is advisable not to leave him on his own with small children. He is not only playful with children, but also shows a great deal of consideration and patience with them. He hardly ever shows any aggressive behaviour and you rarely hear him barking. Perhaps it is his imposing appearance which prevents adversaries from daring to approach, making any barking superfluous. However, if anyone in his pack is in danger, even this peace-loving Newfoundland dog would not hesitate to protect his loved ones.

He loves close contact to his humans and wants to be part of family life. Regular strokes and attention are just as important for him as regular exercise. This big dog does not really feel comfortable with apartment life, he really needs lots of space and is particularly happy near the sea or other waters. You would not be able to pass any stretch of water without allowing him to have a short bath. This intelligent working dog needs fresh air and a lot of exercise every day and that means that his owners must be very active too. He should also be intellectually challenged every day as he is used to solving everyday problems independently.

The Newfoundland is suitable for beginners, due to his quiet and relaxed character. It is important that his training is carried out with loving consistency, a lot of patience and sensitivity. Due to his size, it is important that you set great value in his training. You need to be clear from the start that you will never be able to take a Newfoundland anywhere on the lead if he does not want to go. Therefore, it is imperative that you practice walking him on the lead and calling him back with a great deal of consistency. If he does not obey your commands, you will not be able to control him later. However, with the tips in this handbook, that should not be a problem for you.If you have not yet chosen your Newfoundland, but are only thinking about buying one, I would like to give you the following tip:

It is important to buy him from a reputable breeder and inform yourself about him and his parents. Your Newfoundland will live 9 to 13 years and therefore, it is important that he is healthy and will not have a difficult life from birth onwards because of over-breeding. Look too, at how the breeder treats his own dogs – A red light should be blinking if he keeps them in kennels – and check whether his methods are compatible with those you will be reading about in this book. If a dog has been traumatised by his breeder in early life, it takes an enormous amount of re-programming to correct it, which is too much for most dog owners.

So have a good look at the puppies, their parents and the breeder before you buy one so that you can avoid problems and ensure that you have a long and happy life with your Newfoundland.

- Chapter 2 -

CORNERSTONES OF TRAINING PUPPIES

There are a number of books about training puppies and even more opinions. Almost every dog owner does it differently and you have probably heard a lot of tips from your friends. It would not be unusual for you to wonder, if all this training stuff really needs to be taken so seriously.

The answer to this question is a definite "YES"!

You probably do not live like a hermit. You live in a village or town, which automatically restricts the freedom of your dog. In addition, there are a lot of distractions which can affect him in today's world.

He will come into contact with other dogs, with people and children. You may take him with you when shopping, going into restaurants or while on holiday. You will receive guests and perhaps sometimes leave him alone.

It is important that your Newfoundland is reliable in all those situations. He has to deal with his environment. He should not be afraid of noise, people or new things. He may not react aggressively and must rely completely on you as the leader of the pack.

If he has received good training from you, both of your lives will clearly be more pleasant and relaxed. Your dog will be less stressed and will be able to enjoy more freedom. For example, you can allow your Newfoundland to run without a lead because you know that you can call him back to you at any time. And you will leave your house with a better feeling, without being afraid of what he will get up to this time.

And one more advantage: You will reduce prejudice against badly trained or malicious Newfoundlands and help to promote a better image of owner and dog.

WHAT MUST YOUR NEWFOUNDLAND LEARN?

Most dog owners believe that it is enough if their dog comes to them when they call and if he does not pull on the lead. Those are two very important lessons, but they are not enough by themselves. And, more importantly, calling him back is one of the most demanding exercises of them all. That does not mean that your Newfoundland only needs to run to you if you hold a treat to his nose. You have not mastered calling back until your dog comes to you without complaint when you call him, even while playing with other dogs. In other words, he must leave even the most distracting diversion immediately when you call him. Then you have mastered the call back.

Perhaps you will be laughed at by other dog owners but "a little" obedience is not enough. If you do not make any demands on your dog in everyday life and more or less let him do what he wants, why should he obey you under other circumstances, in particular, when he is playing with other dogs, can smell something interesting or just cannot be bothered?

It is important, that you understand the character of your dog before you begin with puppy training. Particularly with regard to the Newfoundland, you can barely see that they are descended from the wolf, but they are; and wolves live in packs. Despite centuries of breeding, Newfoundlands still maintain their primitive instincts.

That means for you: In a pack there is a clear structure and a defined pecking order. At the head is the pack leader, who has a lot of self-confidence, is willing to take responsibility and always knows what he wants. He maintains discipline and does not accept subordination, not only sometimes, but ever.

If your Newfoundland has the feeling that you are not up to this role, he will take it over. Unfortunately, he cannot properly assess many dangerous situations, which can put him in danger. As an example, not recognising the danger of oncoming traffic or the long-term effects of eating human food on his body. But you can. That is why it is imperative, that you take the role of the pack leader, even if it is difficult and people may make fun of you.

The good news is: The basic training, which your Newfoundland, being an average family dog, must take to heart, is limited. The methods you need are not rocket science and can be mastered by anyone, who has the will to do so.

THE BASICS

In addition to the necessary basic commands of calling back and going back on the lead, here are four more:

Your dog must sit and lie down on command. As an extension, he must be able to do both of these at a distance, even if he cannot see you. He should only move when you allow it. Lastly, your dog should be able to be left alone for a few hours without causing chaos or barking loudly.

He should be capable of carrying out all these commands, not only within your own four walls, but also outside and despite diversions from other people, dogs, loud noises or enticing smells.

If your Newfoundland is also capable of not begging at the table or otherwise for food, not jumping up at people and not chewing things, which do not belong to him, you are both making good progress.

HOW DO YOU ACHIEVE THAT?

Do not worry, you will not have to incessantly punish your dog. This is no longer a part of modern and effective dog training. The training in this guidebook spans two pillars:

Operant and classical conditioning.

Operant conditioning only means that your Newfoundland would prefer to behave in a way for which he receives gratification. At the same time, he would avoid behaviour with which he associates unpleasantness. For example, if he receives a treat when he sits, he associates this with a positive feeling. If he hears a loud, shocking noise while he is contemplating eating your sandwich, he is most likely to avoid that situation next time.

As a conclusion, you will learn, on the following pages, how you can help your dog associate required positive behaviour compared to undesirable negative behaviour. This should of course be done without rebuke and should be based on consequential actions and correct linkage.

On the other hand, there is the classical conditioning with respect to the ability of your Newfoundland to learn by himself. He will watch you and notice those things, which always happen the same way. If he recognises them, he will behave in a certain way. For example, if you always wear the same pair of shoes while taking him for a walk, in time he will not only be happy when you both walk out the door, but already when you put on the shoes.

Classical conditioning shows how important certain rituals and structures are. In this way alone, if you repeat them often enough, it will activate behavioural patterns in your dog.

CONCLUSION

It is not enough to demand obedience sometimes and sometimes not. In order for you and your dog to live happily together, it is necessary for your dog to obey you in all matters. You need to understand his nature and consciously behave as a masterful pack leader.

You will reward good behaviour and use negative links to counter bad behaviour. Using regular rituals, you will enable your Newfoundland to recognise patterns and behave accordingly.

It is important to be consistent, to systemise your lessons, to practice regularly, make constant repetitions and recognise immediately linked behaviour.

- Chapter 3 -

BEFORE THE PUPPY ARRIVES

The preparation begins even before your little Newfoundland arrives. Part of the preparation is to read thoroughly through this guidebook, possibly more than once. After that, you need to make a few decisions in order to lay the groundwork for your relationship. These are as follows:

THE MAIN RELATIONSHIP

The first point to be clear about is who will take the part of the main relationship (the pack leader) for this small animal. The task is high on responsibility, will be time-consuming and will be a challenge. For this reason, it should not be given to a child. Even if it is well-meant, it would not be in the best interests of your Newfoundland. Puppies recognise children more as friends and playmates, but not as pack leaders on whom they can orientate themselves.

The job of the pack leader is not only to assume responsibility for the training of the puppy. The main part of his responsibility is to be masterful and authoritative. The pack leader is responsible for recognising danger well in advance, to ensure all the rules are followed and to project security. In addition, the pack leader is responsible for feeding and taking care of the pack.

Arguably, one of the most difficult exercises is to ensure, that not all demands for action come from your Newfoundland. For example, demands for petting or play. No pack leader would react to such a demand. Even if you would like to, you should not react to it. In a pack, the pack leader decides what is to be done. Most dog-owners unconsciously react almost automatically, when their pet asks to be petted.

As the pack leader, it is important that you are constantly checking your behaviour towards your Newfoundland. As in all things, small errors tend to creep in.

PRIVILEGES

Once the pack leader has been elected, the next step is to decide on privileges. You should decide, prior to your puppy arriving, how you want to structure your relationship with him. This includes what he is allowed to do and what not.

This part is particularly important, if you are not naturally authoritative or are already afraid of your position as pack leader. If that is the case, you need to carefully consider, which privileges are suitable to show him indirectly which rank he has.

Many dog owners do not care about whether their dog eats first or is allowed on the couch or bed. But all these are privileges, which are normally only allowed for the pack leader. Some people may laugh and not understand, but it is more than helpful, when your Newfoundland is only allowed to eat after everyone else is finished. The raised sleeping places are taboo for him, because this is only allowed for the pack leader.

In addition, it is helpful to define rooms, which your Newfoundland is now allowed to enter. This could, for example, be the kitchen, bathroom and/or the bedrooms. You may think these rules are hard, but remember, your dog is not human and he does not think like a human. You send him contradictory signals, if you command obedience one moment and in the next moment allow him to sleep in the pack leader's place, or give him the honour of eating first.

If you send contradictory signals, your Newfoundland will feel insecure. He will start to do what he thinks is right, because he does not have anyone whom he can rely on to guide him. The more he has success, the stronger his behaviour through operant conditioning will be.

Important by privileges and all other rules: They have to be carried out consistently by all family members and any visitors.

THE TIME FACTOR

As the third and last point, you must decide how much time you are willing to invest in your new life partner. Most dog owners underestimate the amount of time necessary to train their puppy, which can lead to bad behaviour later on by their dogs.

So that this does not happen, you should be clear, that good puppy training takes time, lots of time. During the first weeks and months, your little Newfoundland will not be able to spend much time alone. He will probably need to be let out to relieve himself every two hours. Someone must consistently take care, what he is doing, so that he does not pick up any bad habits.

The first weeks are the most important for you and your puppy, so you need to allocate time, a lot of time for him. If you are working, take a few weeks off. What he does not learn early, he will never learn. Whatever you do not teach him at the beginning, it will be more difficult for him to learn later on.

- Chapter 4 -

THE FIRST FEW WEEKS

GETTING YOUR PUPPY TO UNDERSTAND YOU

In order for your training to be successful from the very first day, it is important that your Newfoundland and you speak the same language. Your little dog does not hear what you say, but listens to your voice and watches your body language. For this reason, both should be sending out the right signals. You will learn how to do this now!

Really, it is quite simple: If you want your dog to take notice of you, speak to him with an exciting and happy voice. At the same time, move in a determined and inviting manner. If you want your dog to be quieter, then speak more quietly with him and move more slowly and quietly.

The timing is just as important as the voice and the body language. Despite the beliefs of many dog owners, your Newfoundland will never be able to understand the words you are saying. He makes his own assumptions listening to your voice, watching your body language and in the context of what has happened before.

This means for you: If you want to praise your dog, do it immediately, if he has displayed the required behaviour. The same applies, of course, to negative behaviour. How does that look in practice?

Let us assume that your little puppy has done something wrong and has chewed a shoe. You see it and, incensed, you call him to you. The puppy comes running to you and receives an angry tirade from you, that it is not correct behaviour to chew shoes. What does the puppy learn from this? He learns, that when he runs to you, he will be met with anger. This means that the next time you call him, he will think twice before coming to you. He does not understand the angry words you say to him but he has learned, that you are angry when he comes to you.

The opposite is also true. Your little puppy sits down like a good boy and you want to praise him. But directly after he sits down, he stands up again, after which you give him a treat. How does your puppy link that together? He does not link the treat with sitting down.

Always take care when you praise or rebuke him. This applies naturally not only to puppies but also for your adult Newfoundland.

A small tip: Always take the treats you give him for training from his main meal. In addition, it is recommended that you train with him when he is hungry enough to willingly take part in the exercises. Last but not least, do not get used to feeding him treats for no reason. Your Newfoundland should know from the start that he has to work for them.

GETTING HIM USED TO HIS NEW SURROUNDINGS

The time has come. At last you can collect your Newfoundland from the breeder. It is recommended that you take at least **one more person with you**. This way you can have someone drive the car, for example, while you can look after your new puppy in peace. In addition, you should be well prepared from the start. Take a collar, lead, blanket and perhaps some kitchen paper with you. It is possible, that your little Newfoundland may feel sick.

Depending how long the journey takes, you may need to **take water** with you and after an hour, at the longest, **take a break,** so that he can relieve himself. It would be best if you can arrange to arrive home not too late. This way your Newfoundland has time to have a good look around the house before he has to spend the first night of his life without his siblings and mother.

My **insider tip** would be, to take his blanket to the breeder a few weeks before you pick your puppy up and ask him, if he would lay the blanket out in the puppy area. This has the immense advantage that your little Newfoundland recognises something familiar and which smells of his family. He will feel much more settled, especially at night.

Once he is home, let your little Newfoundland out in the fresh air, either in your own garden or on a field close to your home. Be careful how you choose this place, because many dogs tend to relieve themselves in the same place, so you will be setting the foundation by showing him a "good place". This should not be a place where you like to sit or which the family uses.

After that, go back to your house or apartment. In the first few weeks, it is especially important that your puppy has a **peaceful start** so protect him from too much action. Relatives and friends are also excited about your new family member, but the needs of your four-legged friend are your priority. Allow him to explore his new surroundings intensively for a few days, before you subject him to new stimuli and impressions. There is plenty of time to introduce him to others.

Show him his new home. Show him where to find his food bowl, his blanket – or his personal space – and where his toys are. Watch how he reacts because every dog reacts differently in this very new situation.

Is he tired and does he want to find a quiet space? Is he hungry or thirsty? Perhaps you have a very bold one, who is ready to play. Try to go with his needs and do not pressurise him to do anything. During this introduction period you can check if everything is **"dog proof"** because your puppy will show you within the first few days, if he can reach wires, whether the garden fence has holes in it, or if there are any tempting plants around.

The settling in phase, during the first few weeks, is enough training for your puppy. The only thing you need to practice with him is **getting used to his name**. A lot of people underestimate something, which seems so simple. Your dog does not know, what his name is and does not understand, that some of the sounds, that you make, are meant for him. What he does know is the operant conditioning, which we discussed in the previous chapters.

After you have chosen the right name for him (this should not be too long but clear to pronounce), the conditioning begins. Always say his name in a friendly and happy tone and link it to something positive, for example a stroke. Or you can call his name and show him something interesting, like a toy. This is how your little Newfoundland learns his name without any difficulty and he always links his name to something positive.

Do not make the mistake of using his name without reason and chat unnecessarily much to him. In that way, he loses his grasp of it and you will wonder, why your Newfoundland does not react anymore.

Take Notice: The name of your Newfoundland should only be used sparingly and only linked to something positive. This applies for the whole of his life.

Even more importantly than the unnecessary chatting, beware of negative links. Never reprimand your dog using his name, because he will link his name to something negative. Never shout his name to stop him from doing something. The word for that in puppy training is “no”. If you do not avoid that, your Newfoundland will tend to avoid you automatically, when you call his name. You do not want that, do you?

BUILDING A RELATIONSHIP

I already mentioned at the beginning of this book, how important the pack leader is for your puppy. But how do you become this person? It is not enough just to say it. In order to build the bond, you will need to spend as much time as you can with your puppy. He needs to relate to you, respect you and trust you.

The most proven method to strengthen your bond is to take **bonding walks**. These are carried out only by the pack leader and should not be longer than 5 to 15 minutes in the first 16 weeks. At the beginning it will be enough to take him on one bonding walk per day because you will not want to flood his senses.

The good thing about these walks is, that you can utilise the **following instinct** of your four-legged friend, which is strongest during the first few weeks. A puppy knows instinctively, that he cannot survive alone and because of that, he looks for a protective bond. If you continue with these walks determinedly, he will automatically and intensively learn that he must always be attentive to you.

What does a bonding walk look like at its best?

Take your puppy out into the country. Find a quiet field where your little Newfoundland will not be distracted by other dogs, people, or cars. He should concentrate completely on you. Take him and put him in the middle of the field. Then start walking. Not quickly, but also not too slowly. If your Newfoundland is a little shy, you can encourage him by saying a few happy-sounding words, but please, nothing more.

You will see, he will follow you instinctively. Make sure that he has to try hard to keep up with you and change direction every few yards. Take notice of your own body language. It should show determination and you must not hesitate. Should your puppy walk past you and not take notice of you, you must show him, that this behaviour has consequences. Immediately, change direction, do a 180° turn and walk quickly without hesitation.

Because of his follower instinct, your puppy will start to follow you after a few seconds. As with all exercises, the most important thing is, that you carry them out with consistency. Practise once a day for between 5 and 15 minutes and take notice, of what your puppy is doing. If he is not taking notice of you, then ensure that he does by pursuing the direction change training.

When you are finished with the training, pick him up and carry him back to the car.

In addition to the bonding walks, **exploratory walks** are also good for your Newfoundland. Puppies are naturally inquisitive and Newfoundlands particularly so. Integrate a small nature adventure into your routine. Not only does this improve his motoric skills, but also it will satisfy his innate inquisitiveness.

An example of an exploratory walk would be to wade through a gentle stream or to explore a pile of leaves. Run over a fallen tree trunk with your puppy or balance on a wall. Please be careful not to overwhelm him or force him to do something he does not want to. Should your Newfoundland be afraid, tease him onto the tree trunk with a treat. It is important, that he makes the decision. Here you can also reward small accomplishments and, in this way, introduce him to new things.

The third part of building a bond is grooming. Even though his thin puppy fur does not need much attention, it is recommended to get your bundle of trouble used to brushing. While he is a puppy, a massage glove is enough to massage his skin and fur. Most

Newfoundlands love that and it will make grooming a positive experience for him.

From the beginning, get him used to having his fur, eyes, ears, paws and lips checked regularly, a few times a week. I also recommend that you get him used to you cleaning his paws from very early on, if they are dirty. Repeat it for practice purposes, even if it is not necessary.

If your Newfoundland protests, continue with your routine without hesitation. Stay calm and ignore his defensive behaviour. After a short while he will tolerate it. Naturally, you can reward him at the end with a treat or his toy.

HOW TO GET YOUR PUPPY HOUSETRAINED

One of the first things a dog owner wants is for his dog to be housetrained. Unfortunately, this is where a lot of mistakes are made, which can negatively influence the human-dog relationship permanently. You can read below how to avoid that and teach him what is right and what is a "no go".

As already described in a previous chapter, it is necessary to spend a lot of time with your puppy. Keep him close to you and do not let him out of your sight. As soon as he looks as if he needs to relieve himself (usually he will sniff around a lot and turn in circles), it is urgent, that you bring him outside. Normally, you will not have time to call him, by that time the accident has already happened. Grab him and carry him out.

Praise him profusely, if he relieves himself outside. In addition, it is recommended that you make a sound signal when your puppy relieves himself, for example "go on" or "hurry up". This has the advantage that he will associate this signal with his action. This can be very useful for you, particularly if you are in a hurry.

It is useful to know, that puppies react to certain situations by wanting to relieve themselves. In those cases, you can be proactive and, as a precautionary measure, take him outside. That could be, for example, after eating or playing or when he has just woken up. You should take him out as soon as that activity is finished. The less the dog has the possibility to relieve himself in the house, the quicker he will learn that he should only do it outside.

Do not be surprised if your Newfoundland sometimes makes a "greeting drop", when he gets excited because of visitors arriving. That is perfectly normal. If you know in advance that guests are coming, you should take him to the place, where he can relieve himself directly before they arrive.

In order to avoid that your little Newfoundland has an accident in the night, it is recommended that you let him sleep in a dog box or similar at first. Dogs of all breeds have a problem sleeping where they have had such an accident. Your puppy is no different and he will become restless or even make a sound when he is ready to go out. Once you have achieved that, you have the chance to take him out early enough to prevent accidents. If a puppy needs to go out about every 2 hours during the day, you will see that his rhythm slows down noticeably during the night. Even so, it is possible that you will need to take him out once or twice during the night. Be prepared and have shoes and jacket ready at the door.

The absolute “no go” by training your puppy is to combine scolding with having an accident. Think about what I have often explained before. Your dog is not a human and does not think like a human. He will not understand your punishment or your scolding. If you shout at him for making a puddle in the living room, he will never understand that you are angry because he has done it inside and not outside.

For him the only logical conclusion is: My master is angry because I relieved myself, so I will not do that in his presence anymore. This is something that you never want to permanently ingrain into the sub-conscious of your puppy.

If an accident happens, it happens and you cannot change it. Neither scolding nor praise is suitable in this case. The accident should be cleared up without reaction from you.

THE FIRST COMMANDS

FEEDING

As explained at the beginning of this chapter, you should refrain from training during the first few weeks. After that, you can start training your puppy in small doses. I recommend, as a starting exercise, the systematic setting up of the feeding routine. This exercise has several advantages: Firstly, it increases the bonding with you, because you are responsible for his **feeding**. Secondly, it decreases the danger, that your Newfoundland will defend his food against you and it lays the ground work for the *calling off* command.

It would be best to link this exercise with an indirect rank indication, by always giving your Newfoundland his food after the family has had theirs. When it is time for him to eat, do the following:

1. One member of the family holds the puppy a short distance away from his feeding place.
2. In the meantime, you prepare his food. Make sure he notices you are doing that. As soon as you have his attention,

he will want to come to you. This is an ideal prerequisite for the exercise.

3. When his food is ready, kneel down and hold his food bowl in front of you. As soon as you have taken that position, your family member should let the puppy go. When the puppy moves towards you and the bowl, give him the command “here”.
4. The puppy storms towards you. As soon as he arrives, praise him, put his bowl down in front of you and let him enjoy his food.

Repeat this exercise each feeding time, which is three to four times a day with puppies. The routine and, most importantly, the timing of the command has great significance.

If your puppy has mastered not only this exercise but also the “sit” command, you should add **waiting in front of the food bowl** to the routine.

To do this, repeat points 1 – 3 above exactly as written. Then continue as follows:

4. The puppy storms towards you. This time you do not praise him but give him the command "sit" as soon as he arrives.
5. Put down the food bowl only after he has obeyed the command.
6. Important: The puppy may not eat yet. He must wait a few seconds before you give him the "eat" command.

You should vary the time your puppy has to wait before he is allowed to eat. At the beginning it should only be a few moments. Later, you could do something, like wiping the preparation surfaces, before you let him eat.

If you do this exercise consistently at every meal time, you will achieve a completely different basis for your relationship than most dog owners. I can tell you from my own experience, that most dog owners will ridicule you for this consistency. Some people may even consider it to be cruelty. It is not. Always remember that your Newfoundland is not a human. In the pack, the pack leader gives the signal as to whom can eat and when. For him that is normal.

In addition, you will notice how strong your commitment to each other has become and how he now accepts your authority. After that, you will not have the problem that your dog growls if you want to touch his food, because he knows that you have the sovereignty over him.

SIT

Now we come to the exercise - **sit**. This is not only one of the most important exercises, but also one of the easiest.

1. Hold your hand over your puppy's head with a treat in it. He will probably try to take it from you one way or another. You should not allow that. When he jumps up, close your hand and ignore his behaviour. Stay calm and try not to say anything.
2. When your Newfoundland becomes too tired to hold his head up, he will sit down to make it easier to look up. As soon as he sits down completely, give him the command "sit" and, at the same, time give him his reward.

You will already notice, after a few days, that your dog will understand this exercise. On average, a dog needs to carry out an exercise successfully at least 100 times for him to internalise it permanently.

It is important with all exercises that they are carried out cleanly. If your Newfoundland does not sit down completely, or if he jumps up from the seated position, you must not reward him. Wait a few moments until he sits properly then you can give him his treat.

Sit is a quiet exercise so your voice and your body language should be peaceful.

Sit for advanced training is when you do not stand in front of your little Newfoundland but allow him to sit beside you. This is a little more difficult, but you will benefit from this exercise in everyday life, for example when you have to stand at the roadside, waiting for traffic or when you receive visitors at home.

In order to practice this, hold the treat at your side. If he masters this exercise, let him sit a bit longer before you give him his reward.

LIE DOWN

The next step in the training is the exercise – **lie down**. You should not start this until your Newfoundland has mastered the *sit* exercise and is able to stay in that position for a short period of time. *Lie down* is best practised when your dog is a little tired because then he is happier to lie down than when he is full of energy.

This is how you teach him the *lie down* exercise.

1. Allow your Newfoundland to sit.
2. As soon as he is sitting quietly, hold a treat in front of his nose.
3. Lower the treat, making sure that you stay close to the puppy so that he does not jump up.
4. He will try to reach the treat, so he will follow you down into the lying position.
5. As soon as he is lying completely, give him the command "lie down" and give him his reward.

FINISH EXERCISE

At the same time, you are practising *lie down,* I recommend you to practise **finish exercise.** What do I mean by that?

As I already mentioned, the pack leader decides what is to be done. That is why we spoke in a previous chapter about not reacting to the play wishes of your Newfoundland. Deciding when to stop an activity is equally as important as deciding when to start one. Your Newfoundland should learn from the start that only you can decide what happens when. This applies to petting, playing and also training.

This is how you train *finish exercise* as an example with the *sit* exercise.

6. After you have rewarded your Newfoundland, let him sit again.
7. Then give him the *finish exercise* command by saying “let’s go” and make clear to him with your body language, that he should finish the exercise.

Once you have mastered these basic exercises, you are ready to start with the real training of basic knowledge. You will learn how to do this in the following chapter.

HOW TO AVOID UNDESIRABLE BEHAVIOUR

BITING

Most puppy owners know this problem: Your little rascal is not only rough with the furniture and articles in your home, but also bites when he is playing and frolicking. Although most puppies do not have enough strength to cause injury, their sharp teeth can easily cause small cuts.

Particularly on the subject of biting, it is important, that you know from the start that your little Newfoundland is not being vicious. Up to now, he has been able to develop freely without many rules and does not understand taboos. It is your job in the next few weeks to show him what taboos and which rules he needs to know, carefully and slowly.

Up to now, your Newfoundland has been able to bite hard into his siblings and shake the fur wildly, without injuring them. It is normal for him to behave like that. Now you need to teach him, that he could injure others, particularly children, with this behaviour.

You can do this in one of two ways. The first method is particularly suitable for sensitive dogs, who place great importance on your affection towards him. As soon as your Newfoundland begins to play, using his teeth, stop what you are doing immediately. Ideally, you would stand up, turn your back on him and walk a few steps away from him. If you like, you can let out a small cry of pain, the moment he bites.

This would be enough for many puppies. They quickly learn, that biting leads to a break in the great game they were playing and that they will be ignored. For a lot of dogs, this is hardly bearable.

There are some dogs, however, where this method will not be enough. If you seem to have got yourself a wild one who, despite consistent ignoring and breaking up of the game, still insists on happily biting, you will need to increase the pressure.

You must understand that, even when puppies are playing with each other, they are not allowed to do everything they want. If one of them goes too far, he will be put in his place using a muzzle grip. This is often used by the mother of the puppies and is very effective. When applied to us humans, it means that as soon as your Newfoundland playfully bites, you should hold his muzzle for a short while. You can emphasise this by substituting the growl of the mother with a signal word, such as “bad” or “taboo”.

Use this method consistently and you will see how your puppy will stop biting. Be patient and do not expect too much from your Newfoundland. It could take a little longer than you would like, even if you are consistent. Do not lose patience with him or lose your motivation, if your puppy starts to bite again after a short while. That is normal. It is important that you stay on the ball and remain consistent.

JUMPING UP

Jumping up, just like biting, is normal behaviour for your puppy, until he knows, that you do not want it. It is important, that you teach your sweet puppy, that jumping up is taboo, so that it does not turn into a permanent behavioural pattern.

The procedure for this is very similar to the one you would use to prevent biting:

- Turn away from your Newfoundland the next time he jumps up.
- Wait until he stops jumping up before beginning the next activity (greeting, rewarding, playing, feeding etc.).
- Under no circumstances, should you take notice of him. That means no eye contact, no speaking (at all if you can) and no active touching from your side.

This should work with most puppies, if you are consistent and apply the same procedure with everyone who comes into contact with your Newfoundland.

If your Newfoundland still does not stop jumping up, you can add a signal word, such as "bad" or "taboo". However, I recommend that you do not use these signal words from the beginning. This can cause the jumping up to continue in some dogs.

If you are not able to prevent your Newfoundland from jumping up, try using a distraction. However, I recommend exhausting both other methods before trying this and use only when your patience is at an end. For this, your dog will need to be very familiar with the command "sit", otherwise it will not work.

As soon as your Newfoundland jumps up the next time, give him the command "sit". He cannot do both things at the same time. Once he has done what you ask, praise him lavishly. Repeat the exercise every time your Newfoundland jumps up. If your puppy does not immediately obey, it could be that he is not yet familiar enough with the command "sit". Keep practising the command "sit" with him, even if he is not jumping up. Add more distractions. Once "sit" works reliably, you can use it again to prevent jumping up.

RESTLESSNESS

Most puppies are very lively and alert and are not able to gauge for themselves when they need a rest. If you try to play with them until they are tired, they become like small children, who become even more restless and whiny. They do not understand it, therefore it is important that you decide when your puppy should rest and show him how to know when it is time to stop.

For this, your Newfoundland will need a place in your home where he can retreat. I recommend using a dog box for this, but of course it will also work with a blanket or basket. The important thing is, that everyone accepts, that this is his space and he should not be disturbed when he retreats.

How do you do this best? For one thing, you can train him passively by using the signal word "easy" or "sleep" when your puppy is relaxed and nearly asleep. This is a question of timing and consistency.

You can add this onto a session with active training. After a short walk (about 10 minutes) you can go into a relaxation phase. Go with your puppy to his box and start to stroke him slowly and peacefully, perhaps even to massage him a little. Even when he is still a bit wild and wants to play, you should remain peaceful and continue with the relaxation techniques.

As soon as you see that your Newfoundland is becoming more relaxed and quieter, you can use the signal word "easy" or "sleep".

After several days or weeks, depending on how quickly your Newfoundland learns, he will react properly to the relaxation signal word. In this way, you will be able to calm him down after experiencing a stressful event.

It is important, that you get used to using the relaxation signal word in other situations, not only when your puppy has been particularly active, otherwise the word can lose its meaning. Use it prudently every time you give him a relaxed stroke.

FEAR OF RIDING IN CARS

These days, it is very important that your Newfoundland is able to cope stress-free with being driven in a car. Some dogs have no problems right from the start, but others are afraid, even of getting into the car, or they vomit regularly during the drive.

In order to avoid that with your Newfoundland, you need to get him used to your car at a very early age. The best way is to let his experience with your car be a pleasant one, right from the beginning, even while it is still stationary. For example, you can sit with him in the boot and stroke him or give him his favourite treat. It is important that he associates positive thoughts with the car. It depends upon each individual how long this process takes. Some puppies have no fear at all but it may take others days or weeks before they step into even a stationary car, without fear.

Once this step has been overcome, I recommend that you test how your puppy reacts, once the engine is running. If he remains quiet, everything will be alright. However, if he becomes unsettled, you will need to get him used to this phase, again with regular strokes and treats. Repeat this step until your puppy can lie relaxed in the boot or the back of the car.

After that, you can travel a few yards backwards and forwards. How does your Newfoundland react? If he remains quiet, you could take a run around the block. If he gets upset, take it slowly and repeat the rolling backwards and forwards phase until he becomes quiet.

If your dog tends to vomit in the car, I recommend never feeding him directly before travelling. Just like us humans, there are animals whose stomachs turn over during car journeys. In such cases, your Newfoundland should have eaten at least two hours before you take him out in the car.

What else do you need to bear in mind with car journeys?

- Ensure that he has a safe seat. I recommend a dog box in the boot of your car. Alternatively, you can use a dog guard, a non-slip mat or a safety belt for dogs.
- Take the lead off your dog, so that he cannot get stuck or hang himself.
- Never leave your dog alone in the car, particularly in warm temperatures. The amount of heat in the car is often underestimated.

- Plan regular breaks in your journey, at least one every two hours. Give your Newfoundland the opportunity to drink something, relieve himself and move around.
- Teach your Newfoundland early, that he is not allowed to leave the car without your permission, that reduces danger significantly.

DESTRUCTIVENESS

I am sure there is no puppy owner who cannot complain, that their little rascal had destroyed something. This behaviour is perfectly normal, but it is important to ensure, that it does not become the rule. It is up to you to teach your Newfoundland, that he should not be playing with your shoes, only with his own toys.

The first step is to ensure, that your puppy does not have the opportunity to chew something which he is not supposed to. Put everything, which he is not allowed to touch, up and out of his reach. This includes shoes, vases and wires, as well as rugs, long curtains and tablecloths.

The second step is to distract your puppy from doing anything he is not supposed to do, before he starts. You will need to be extremely attentive and consistent. If you see, that he is starting to chew the table leg, pick him up without comment, put him down somewhere else and then start to play an interesting game with him with his favourite ball. You show him this way, that there are better and more interesting things to do than chewing the table leg. You will probably have to do this several times before your Newfoundland understands.

He will keep trying to do things which you do not want him to do. Then it is your job to remain patient and consistent, and divert his attention to more interesting things

This method works for most dogs. If your dog does not react to your wishes after several weeks of consistent distraction, you can begin to use signal words, such as "taboo" or "bad" and, if necessary, use the muzzle grip technique.

But what do you do if your puppy is always quiet in your presence but turns into a vandal the moment you turn your back?

Here too, the first step is to take away everything which may cause devastation. Secondly you need to find out why he has so much destructive energy. Mostly, it is because your puppy has not had enough exercise.

I recommend in such a case to occupy your puppy intensively before leaving him alone. You could take him out for a walk, play a game with him or tire him out with some training, for example teaching him new commands. After that, you should go into the peaceful routine. Allow him to wind down. If you do this consistently, your Newfoundland will not have enough energy to get up to mischief and ideally will sleep during your absence.

Please do not expect, that your vandal will turn into a docile puppy after one training session. It takes time and a lot of training, repetition and patience from your side, for him to settle into the required behaviour.

Punishing your puppy when you come home from being out will not have the required effect. On the one hand, your puppy will not associate his wrong-doing with your punishment and on the other hand, he does not understand what he has done wrong.

- Chapter 5 -

TRAINING BASIC KNOWLEDGE

Congratulations!

You have achieved a lot with your little Newfoundland once you have reached the *training basic knowledge* stage. You have lain the foundation and you will see, that the rest is not so difficult, as you are a well-coordinated team and your Newfoundland knows, who is the boss.

In this chapter you will learn the 7 basics I believe every dog owner and every one of their dogs should know off by heart. So that this works for you, below you will learn how to do this step by step.

Let's do it!

WALKING ON THE LEAD

Every dog owner wishes that he had trained his dog consistently to walk well on the lead, but very few are ready to put in the work necessary. This applies particularly to owners of large breeds, to which the Newfoundland belongs. In comparison to a 4 lb dog, which any child can hold, despite him pulling on the lead, your four-legged friend will develop enormous strength. If this strength is not under control – your control – this could lead to dangerous situations, not only for you and your Newfoundland but also for third persons. This is why lead leadership is the most important thing when walking your little Newfoundland.

There is another reason why you should never let your dog pull on the lead and in principle it is always the same reason. Only the pack leader decides where the pack is going. If your dog is pulling on the lead and you allow it, that means for your Newfoundland, that he is deciding the route. If you continue to allow him to gain the authority it is unclear to him why he should take notice of you in other things. You can see that this is a recurring theme throughout the training.

In addition to the above, the operant conditioning already mentioned in this book will ensure that when your puppy is successful in pulling you, you allow him to be the leader, so he will continue to do it. Once he has linked that together, it will be very difficult for you to change his behaviour. Particularly by Newfoundlands, these links are often forged much quicker than their owners would like. Always remember the operant conditioning works in both positive and negative senses.

I would suggest: Please take your lead leadership seriously. You could improve the image of the Newfoundland sustainably when people see that your dog does not pull on the lead. You will discover below how to do this:

1. Walk with your puppy on the lead. If he sees something interesting, he will start to pull in a particular direction.
2. Stand still immediately and do not react. Do not speak to your Newfoundland, just wait.
3. Your Newfoundland may not react immediately, but after a while he will change his behaviour. Perhaps he will

sit down or come running to you. You should continue walking only after he has loosened the tension on the lead.

4. When he has loosened the tension, give him the command "slowly". If you repeat this often enough, he will link the action with the command.
5. Important: As soon as he starts to pull again, stand reactionless until the lead loses tension again.

You need a lot of patience for this exercise. Your little Newfoundland will often pull on the lead, at the beginning as soon as he sees, smells or hears something interesting. It is up to you to ensure, that when the tension increases, you react immediately. The work you invest in this will be rewarded for the rest of your dog's life. There is nothing more pleasant, than a relaxed walk with your dog, without having to fight for control.

WALKING TO HEEL

Once your Newfoundland has learned to walk on the lead, the next step is to master the command "heel". What is the difference between lead leadership and "heel"? While you are practising lead leadership, the goal is that your dog does not pull on the lead. "Heel" is much more. This is when your Newfoundland pays attention to you all the time and walks next to you with a loose lead at all times. It makes no difference whether you turn a corner, stand still or step over an obstacle, your dog will stay in step with you.

As puppies and young dogs generally cannot go for any length of time to *heel*, good lead leadership is very important.

However, before you begin to practice this new command, you should decide which side your dog should walk on. It is not recommended to keep changing sides, it is better to be consistent.

It is up to you, which side you choose. I personally prefer the left side. Why? Because of the traffic. If you are often walking along busy roads, that could be useful. Even the best-trained dog can scare on hearing sudden noises and could do something unexpectedly. If he is walking on your right, this could mean that he inadvertently pushes you and you both end up in the road. I do not need to describe here what that can mean. That said, it is only my personal opinion, there is no specific "better" side.

If you should also decide on the left side you should have his treats in your left jacket pocket. You hold the lead with the right hand. If you decide on the right side, just do the opposite.

This is how you start training:

1. To ensure that your Newfoundland stays at your side, you should keep his attention on you. You can do this best with treats. Entice your Newfoundland to the side you want him to walk on.
2. As soon as he directs his full attention to the treat, start walking determinedly and quickly. Give the command "heel".
3. While you are walking, continue occasionally to say the command.

4. After a short while (after a few meters with puppies), let him sit and give him the treat as his reward.

During the whole exercise it is acceptable if your puppy tries to lick or nibble the treat. One thing he should not do is to jump up. Choose the distance for this exercise based on the span of his attention. At the beginning this will be very short and you should not overdo it.

If you are able to do this exercise without problems, you can try to do it without the treat. At the beginning, it is recommended to keep your hand in your pocket where the treats are but, after a while, you can let your arm hang down. If your Newfoundland is walking attentively by your side, reward him with a treat. Slowly you should extend the time between rewards.

The following points should also be noted:

- Vary your route and do not just walk straight ahead. Walk in curves or sometimes backwards. Walk quicker or slower. You could perhaps run down a flight of stairs or step over a tree trunk.

Your Newfoundland should stay at your side at all times during these variations.

- As soon as you notice that your puppy has become distracted, motivate him by speaking with an excited voice. The rest of the time it is recommended to say as little as possible, so that his attention is not diluted. Should your little friend stand still or try to go in a different direction, ignore his behaviour and continue walking at a good pace. As soon as he directs his full attention towards you and walks beside you, praise him.
- If your Newfoundland continues to sniff around or to walk too quickly, walk in tight circles with him being on the inside. In this way, you obstruct his path and prevent him from sniffing. Here too, as soon as he directs his full attention towards you, you should praise him.

CALLING YOUR DOG

We already laid the foundation for calling your dog in the previous chapter about feeding. You remember, that your Newfoundland is held by a second person while you prepare his food. As soon as you are in position with his bowl, as he is freed and runs towards you, you give him the command “here”.

If your dog responds by running towards his food without a problem, you can increase the difficulty of the exercise a little. Now you can start to call him in-between feeding times and without him being held by another person. Before you start, you should ensure that he will not be distracted, or was just sleeping. Attract his attention to you with excitement in your voice. Give the command “here” while he is already on his way to you.

If you can master this exercise within your own four walls without difficulties, you can try it outside. Ideally, this would be on your balcony or in your garden. If this works well over a longer period of time, you can increase the difficulty a second time by leaving the garden.

I have a few **secret tips** for you to ensure that the *calling* exercise really works.

- Practice the *calling* command at least three weeks each in your house, in your own garden or balcony and ensure that there are no distractions. The success your puppy experiences during this time will be engrained firmly in his subconscious.
- Ensure, that you draw your dog's attention with an excited voice, before you call him. Only give the command "here" when you are sure that he is coming to you and is relatively close to you. After that you can increase the distance in stages.
- In order to increase his wish to come to you, you can systematically move further away from him, when you draw his attention.
- Ensure that your Newfoundland is hungry when you train this technique, particularly when you are away from the house or garden. Should he feel a

little hunger, he will be particularly keen to react to a treat.

If you follow these tips and systematically build up the exercise, you will experience a lot of success: Your Newfoundland will come directly to you, when you call him without you having to offer him treats.

Once you have mastered this exercise, you should start to prepare distractions for him. This could be playing children, other dogs or an interesting smell. Despite all these distractions, your little four-legged friend should come to you immediately when you call him. It is particularly useful to use your puppy's hunger to your advantage, when teaching this exercise.

At the beginning of the exercise, it is not yet necessary to make your dog sit after he has come to you. This would lead to your puppy thinking that the treat is connected to the *sit* command and not to the *calling.* As soon as the training is going well and you are experiencing some success, you can start to use the *sit* command, after the Newfoundland has received his treat. After countless repeats and preferably not starting until your Newfoundland is no longer a puppy, you can let him sit before he receives his treat.

STAY

Once your Newfoundland has mastered the *stay* exercise, you will notice that everyday life with him is easier and more relaxed. You may be asking yourself why, as many dog owners do not see any value in this exercise. The answer is simple: If you have taught your dog to wait patiently for you, you could let him out of your sight for a few moments without being afraid, that he will run away or get up to mischief. This is helpful when he returns from a walk covered in dirt and you allow him to sit quietly at the front door while you get a towel. Or he could sit outside the pharmacist, while you are inside buying something.

This is how you train the *stay* command:

1. Allow your Newfoundland to "sit" or "lie down" next to you
2. Once he is sitting or lying, relaxed, you say "stay" and stand directly in front of him. At the beginning, just stay in front of him for a few moments. Hold the lead in your hand during this exercise to correct any bad behaviour that might occur. Ensure that the lead is not tight.

3. Go and stand beside him again and praise him.

Once you can do this exercise without mistakes, increase the difficulty. You can do that by increasing the time you stand in front of your Newfoundland. If he can stay at least one minute, quietly sitting, you can raise the difficulty again. Now you can go a few meters away from him, at first only for a short time, then for longer. If he manages to sit quietly and relaxed for at least 2 minutes at the full length of his lead, you have mastered the first milestone.

Your dog is now able to sit where he is told to without being distracted. To add another degree of difficulty, you can add a small amount of distraction to the exercise. You do not stand still in front of him but walk parallel to your Newfoundland, up and down. Not for long, at first, and not far away. After a while, you can increase both distance and length of time.

If he is able to carry out this exercise, you can walk in semicircles and eventually in full circles around him. Once this does not cause him any problems, you can go onto the big challenge: Go out of his range of view for a short time. I recommend you give him the *lie down* command before you do that. Particularly with this exercise, I would recommend that you start with very short periods of time and distances, which you can increase as time goes by.

Here are a few **secret tips** to master the exercise even better:

- The exercises "stay" and "sit" are quiet training times. Your body language and voice should therefore be peaceful.
- To make it easier for your Newfoundland to wait for you, it is a good idea to tire him out first. If he is full of energy, it is difficult for him to stay in one place or in the same position.
- Do not start this exercise until your dog can lie, relaxed, beside you for least 2 minutes.
- At the beginning, always train on the lead with him, but let it hang loosely, as described above. If your Newfoundland stands up during the exercise, it is probable that the time was too long or the distance too great. Take him back to the exact place, that he was sitting or

lying, and repeat the exercise from the beginning.

- Remember, the exercise is not finished until you are standing next to your Newfoundland again. Allow him to sit up before you give him his reward. This detail is particularly important with the exercise *lie down* because your dog will be tense during the exercise. Once he knows that he must lie until you are standing next to him, he can relax a little.
- Carry out this exercise for a few weeks in the *sit* position after which you can sometimes call him to you from the *stay* position.
- Be aware of the timing of the reward. Do not hold a treat in the hand all the time because your puppy will find it even more difficult to wait for the calling command. It will be even more difficult for him, if you take the treat out of your pocket while you are walking

towards him. Wait until you are standing beside him. Often, it is enough just to praise your dog after the exercise.

SIT AT A DISTANCE

At first, many people think that "sit at a distance" is the same as the exercise "stay" while sitting. However, it is not the same. *Sit at a distance* is the highest level of difficulty with respect to the classical *sit* command. This exercise is particularly helpful if you and your Newfoundland suddenly have to stop and it is important that he is able to remain in a particular place, as soon as you give the command, even if you are not with him.

For example, it is possible that a jogger or bike rider suddenly appears and your Newfoundland has gone a little ahead of you; or he has to cross over a street when you call him. In these situations, you can avoid danger, if your Newfoundland sits and obediently waits for you. This is really an advanced exercise, however, and should not be trained at puppy age. I wanted to tell you about it anyway because I think it is very important to know.

This is how you build up your exercise systematically:

1. When you use the command “sit”, stretch your arm outwards and upwards as a *listen* signal.
2. As soon as you think your dog has linked the combination of voice and arm, practice using the command only with the arm. If your Newfoundland sits down competently when commanded, you can start to increase the distance.
3. If your four-legged friend finds himself a few meters away from you, without any distractions, draw his attention towards you. As soon as he stops and looks at you, give him the arm signal. After he has sat down, walk slowly towards him and reward him.
4. Once this exercise is carried out competently, you can increase the distance.
5. If the exercise is also successful at a distance, start training the exercise again at shorter distances, this time with distractions. Once he is competent with this exercise, despite distractions, you can increase the distance a little at a time.

When you have mastered this exercise, you will not only have the benefit that your dog will sit at a distance, but also you will experience, that your dog will look much more in your direction and want to make eye contact. You will notice an increase in the strength of your bond with your dog.

GIVING SOMETHING UP

Many dog owners connect the command "leave" with scolding for bad behaviour by their dog. As with previous exercises, the real intention of this command is to invoke a particular behavioural pattern from your puppy. Examples of this are, if you want your Newfoundland to drop a toy or slipper or even a bone, which he has in his mouth.

It is obvious to most why this command is useful in everyday life. However, it is particularly important to me, that this exercise is not connected with fear, but that your dog will learn, through consistency, targeted training and well-timed reward.

You will find out how to do it following the steps below:

1. Your Newfoundland is holding something in his mouth, that he is not supposed to.
2. Instead of shouting at him, lure him towards you using an excited voice.
3. As soon as he reaches you, offer him an exchange. This could either be his favourite toy or a treat.

4. Once he has dropped the item, give him the command “leave”.
5. Repeat this exercise as often as you can. Soon he will let the item go, when you give the command, without you having to offer him something.

Another, longer method is to say “leave” every time your puppy drops something by himself. This demands a lot of attention from you, because you must really do it every time.

You should never make this mistake: Never run after your dog, when he is supposed to drop something. Running after him would cause your Newfoundland to associate, that he has to hide his prey from you, which would make it even more difficult to break this habit. Apart from that, the little guy is much quicker and more agile than you are.

PUTTING THE LEAD ON AND TAKING IT OFF

Putting the lead on and taking it off is another example of an exercise, which is completely neglected by most dog owners. They do not see any sense or added value in building up a systematic routine for this. At the same time, they become angry when their dogs become impatient and do not want their leads taken off or put it on.

If you want to avoid this from happening, you should get your puppy used to the following routine from the beginning, whenever you take his lead off.

1. Use the command *sit* every time you want to put on or take off his lead.
2. Once you have taken his lead off or put it on, let him sit in front of you for a few moments.
3. Wait until he is quiet and, ideally, makes eye contact with you.
4. Only then you should allow him to go, using the command “go on”.

The main point of this exercise is to make your Newfoundland wait quietly and to gain his attention. If his attention wanders and he pulls away from you before you give the command, you are rewarding the wrong behaviour. You already know, without me telling you, what the consequences are of allowing this link to form in his subconscious.

My tip: Hold your little friend inconspicuously by the collar when you take off his lead. If he wants to escape before you allow it, you can immediately slow him down and hold him back. Avoid at all costs, providing him with an undesirable sense of achievement.

- Chapter 6 -

SPECIAL CHAPTER – THE HUNTING INSTINCT

With your Newfoundland you have chosen a dog that usually does not have a strong hunting instinct. So it may sound strange that I have included a special chapter on hunting instincts in this book. But in every race there are individuals who have some characteristics more or less pronounced. For this reason, I have added an extra chapter to this book. Unfortunately, I had to experience as a child an event where our German Shepherd attacked a sheep, which was caught in a fence.

The cries of the sheep in pain and all that blood were bad enough, but my fear, that it could happen again, was even worse. I do not wish this experience to happen to anyone, so I am writing below, what you can do to minimise the danger.

The best method to avoid that your dog becomes a hunter, is to prevent it in the first place. At the time, we made the mistake not to deal with those instincts. Our dog, Sally, began very early to chase after wild animals. We tolerated it, because she was never successful. That was our mistake, because hunting is self-rewarding behaviour.

What does that mean? It means that your dog does not need to be successful in the hunt in order to satisfy his hunting instinct. It is enough for him to follow a trail or a quickly moving object. As soon as he has gained that experience, it works like a drug. He will want to experience this highlight again and again.

Perhaps you are asking yourself how to deal with this. In this chapter, I will explain some preventative measures you can take. Choose the one which fits both of you best. However, whatever you do, one thing is the most important one: Until you can rely on your dog to obey you, you will need to always(!)keep him on the lead in places where there is wildlife. Always remember: Every hunt, whether successful or not, strengthens the compulsion of your Newfoundland to have more! As long as he is on the lead, he will not be tempted nor able to hunt.

Now we come to the measures.

KEEP HIM BUSY

Your Newfoundland is a real bundle of energy. If he is not kept busy, he will develop an unbelievably high energy potential. The more energy your dog has, the more he will react to tempting stimuli, to get rid of it.

For this reason, it is particularly important to keep hunting dogs occupied. I do not only mean physical exercise, although this is an important part. The mental training of your dog is much more important. You will also experience, that your little dog will be exhausted, even after you have done only a few minutes of basic training with him.

If you are intending to go with your Newfoundland to an area, which is full of hunting possibilities, be sure to plan some taxing mental training into your schedule before you go. That will ensure that he has less energy for hunting. You can achieve the same effect by organising a playful treat hunt through your home.

BE PREPARED TO DISTRACT

You have purposely chosen a potential hunter for a pet. For this reason, you should get used to looking around you during every walk. Of course, you can talk to someone but you need to be scanning your surroundings at the same time. Perhaps you are asking yourself why?

You need to recognise potential prey before your Newfoundland does. When you are first to see it, you have a small window of opportunity to distract him before he sees it. Take his favourite toy or a particularly tasty treat with you, when you go out.

If, for example, you see a deer ahead, standing in a clearing, start immediately to play a pulling game with your four-legged friend, throw a ball (in the opposite direction of course) or make him "sit" for a tasty treat. The important thing is, that you make yourself more interesting than chasing a deer would be.

STUDY ALTERNATIVE BEHAVIOUR

We have already spoken about classical conditioning. This is also a good way to counteract the hunting instinct. My dog knows, for example that he must come back to me and walk to heel, if ever a bike rider, jogger or a car approach.

How did I manage that? Simple! I have consistently drummed into him that, if anything approaches us, he needs to come back to me. At the beginning I always had to use the command “here” followed by “heel”. However, Newfoundlands are clever animals. Just as they can recognise the link between “hiking boots” and “walkies”, they can link “jogger approaching” with “here” and “heel”.

It is important that you always demand this behaviour, not only sometimes. If you are consistent, you will be surprised how quickly your four-legged friend learns this lesson.

REINFORCE OBEDIENCE

The basis for all these measures is the same: Your dog must obey you, not only sometimes if he feels like it, but in every situation. You must be able to call him whenever you want to. Also, the command *sit at a distance* is a useful tool to use with your hunt-happy friend.

Often it is much easier to stop your Newfoundland from moving, if he is a long way from you, than it is to bring him back. If he sits at your command, you have the possibility of walking towards him and either distracting him or putting him back on the lead.

Until you are sure that your dog will obey you, you should always keep him on the lead. You can use extra-long leads for training purposes, which can allow your dog to be 10-20 meters away from you. This way, you can always hold your dog back if he wants to hunt.

- Chapter 7 -

CHECK LIST FOR THE START

There is a lot to consider when settling your little Newfoundland into his new home, particularly when he is your first dog. Below are some checklists so that you do not forget anything and so that you can make a perfect start.

There is a lot to think about and take care of, so that you fulfil the criteria necessary to make for a happy dog and owner life. Take a look through the lists to ensure, that you have not forgotten anything.

Firstly, I will show you the most important things that you need to clarify before you even decide upon taking a puppy. Once you have made the decision, I will show you what to watch out for when buying your dog, which formalities are important and what should be on your shopping list, to ensure you have everything you need for the start. Lastly, I will give you a checklist to check whether your environment is puppy-safe and that nothing can happen to your new companion.

PRELIMINARY CONSIDERATIONS

Before you decide to bring a Newfoundland into your life, there are some things you need to consider. You should clarify these points before buying a puppy to ensure, that you can give him a breed-appropriate and happy life. If you are unsure that all points are honestly and unconditionally fulfilled, perhaps it would be better to wait a while before taking that step, while making your preparations. A Newfoundland is not an easy dog!

- ☐ Are you ready to have a dog with you for the next years and to look after him?
- ☐ Is your present home the right place for a Newfoundland? Do you have enough space?
- ☐ Does your present lifestyle (e.g. your job, your holidays, your social environment etc.) fit with having a dog? What will you do with your dog when you are away from your home for a longer period?
- ☐ Are you ready to bring up your puppy as described in this book, to enable you

both to live happily together? Are you strong enough to stand up to those sweet doggy-eyes and to say “no” if it is necessary (and it will often be necessary!)?

- ☐ Do you have time every day (!) to look after your Newfoundland?
- ☐ Can you afford to buy the puppy, initial equipment, food, vet's visits, tax, insurance etc.? A Newfoundland is not a cheap dog, the costs can run into thousands!
- ☐ Have you checked if anyone in your family is allergic to dog-hairs?
- ☐ Have you clarified who will do which jobs in the family and are all the family members in agreement?
- ☐ If you are in rented accommodation, have you checked if dogs are allowed?
- ☐ Are you physically fit and healthy enough to care for a Newfoundland for his whole life? Remember that Newfoundlands can live for up to 15 years.

- ☐ Do you realise that dogs make a lot of mess at home and leave hair everywhere (and by everywhere, I really mean everywhere!)?
- ☐ Are you prepared to look after your Newfoundland round the clock (even at night) while he is a puppy? Have you made a plan how you will do that during the first few weeks?

BUYING YOUR DOG

Before and during the purchase of a dog, it is possible to make a lot of mistakes which will come back to bite you later, including the danger of supporting the breeding of illegal and inappropriately held dogs. In addition, there are several preparations to make in order to find the right dog for you and make a good start.

- ☐ Have you done enough research about the Newfoundland breed, checked the breeder in the internet and found a trustworthy breeder?
- ☐ Have you considered whether it should be a male or female?
- ☐ Have you already thought of a name for your little rascal?
- ☐ While you are with the breeder, there a several points to consider: How do the puppies look and behave? Is the mother present and is she looking after her puppies? Does the breeder offer other breeds for sale (not a good sign!)? What does the environment around the

puppies look like? Is the vendor asking questions about the future life of the puppy and does he seem interested in the welfare of the dog? Is the price realistic or surprisingly low (this could be another sign, that something is wrong)? Are you receiving full information about feeding during the next few weeks and how old the puppy should be before he starts climbing stairs, etc.?

- ☐ Is there a written purchase agreement containing the necessary information regarding vendor, liability issues, sales price, handover, etc.?
- ☐ Have you planned-in several visits to the breeder to find out if you and your Newfoundland puppy are suited to each other?
- ☐ How will you transport your new companion from the breeder to your home? Is your dog familiar with car travel? Do you have something handy to clean up the car, just in case?

FORMALITIES:

When purchasing your puppy, there are several formalities and other paperwork, which need to be done. This is important to avoid unwanted (and expensive) surprises. Here are the most important points, that you need to observe:

- ☐ The purchase of a third-party liability insurance is an absolute necessity (in case your dog causes damage to a third party or even injures someone because he runs into someone's bike, for example, causing the rider to stumble).
- ☐ Punctual registration for dog taxes at the appropriate authority.
- ☐ Checking the environmental requirements around your home (often there are rules about keeping your dog on a lead, as an example).
- ☐ Find a good veterinary surgeon. Research in the internet and ask around your friends for recommendations. When you have found one, check what

vaccinations and examinations are necessary.

- ☐ Find out where the urgent care for your dog is situated, in case something unexpected happens (such as sickness or an accident).
- ☐ Find a good dog school in your area and register your Newfoundland as soon as you can.
- ☐ Sometimes a dog-handler permit is necessary to keep a dog. Find out from the local authorities if you will need one. This would need to be done before you purchase your puppy.

SHOPPING LIST

You will need some basic equipment in order to give your Newfoundland a good home. Unfortunately, you can end up paying a lot of money, but it is inevitable and must be done before your new friend comes home. I recommend obtaining the following articles:

- ☐ A bowl each for food and water (possibly with adjustable height)
- ☐ Harness (make sure it is the right size) and two short leads for puppies (as a reserve). Optionally, a long lead, at least 5m in length, will give your puppy a little more freedom.
- ☐ A dog basket with soft lining to use as a retreat
- ☐ A transport box which fits in your car (or a dog safety belt)
- ☐ A dog brush (or comb)
- ☐ Toys
- ☐ Puppy food (check the type with your breeder and/or vet) and treats
- ☐ A food bag
- ☐ A chewing bone

- ☐ Guards for doors and stairs to prevent your puppy from climbing the stairs to soon or from running out of the house.
- ☐ Tick tweezers
- ☐ Poo bags

PUPPY-SAFE ENVIRONMENT

You should ensure, that the environment in which your puppy lives is safe to prevent him from injuring himself, and also to prevent him from damaging the furniture. This includes the following:

- ☐ Decide which areas of your home your dog is not allowed to enter. You could perhaps separate it off, using a guard. (My dogs are not allowed in the bath-room or kitchen, for example).
- ☐ If you have a garden, make sure it is escape-safe. Do not underestimate how small a hole your puppy can fit through!
- ☐ Put child-safe guards on plugholes, which your puppy could reach.
- ☐ If possible, hide all lose cables.
- ☐ Put away anything breakable, which is within reach of your puppy and any-thing he can knock over.
- ☐ Make sure there are no poisons (e.g. chemicals or plants) inside or outside which he can reach.

- ☐ Put away throw rugs if they end up becoming dog toilets.

Find a suitable place for the dog basket (not too far away from the family but quiet enough to become a refuge).

- Chapter 8 -

CONCLUSION

Congratulations!

You have taken the first step, one which not every dog owner is prepared to do. You have informed yourself comprehensively about the training of your Newfoundland and will be able to build a much more contented and relaxed relationship with your four-legged friend than most people.

This is because you know what is most important:

- You know the difference between humans and dogs as pack animals. You will not be intimidated, when acquaintances laugh at you, only because your dog has to wait for his food, because you know why you are doing it.
- You have taken to heart the importance of consistency in the training of your dog. That is, why you take care with everything you do and question his

behaviour continually. You know, that mistakes creep in, slowly and quietly, without you noticing and you want to avoid that.

- You know, that many things, which seem unimportant to humans, could have an indirect consequence to your puppy's ranking in the family. This includes the order of eating; who is allowed to go where and who decides where to go. You use this knowledge to keep constant and safe control over your puppy and he needs to know that, to become a confident, relaxed and contented dog.
- You know about both operant and classical conditioning and know how to use them when training your Newfoundland. You know which role, both negative and positive, this training has on your dog, so you are able to prevent him from gaining a sense of achievement for something you do not want him to do.

- You know how to train basic elements with your puppy in easy stages. You know, that it is not enough only to expect obedience sometimes and not others and you know how this training will benefit both of you.
- You know, that training puppies has nothing to do with brutal enforcement but is a product of commitment to systematic exercises, good training, countless repeats and loads of patience.
- You know, that the many rules your Newfoundland has to learn, will not harm him but, on the contrary, will help him to understand your world. You give him a home, which he can see as his pack and ensure systematic routines and pecking orders, which he needs. You give him security and leadership.
- Through consistent and loving care for your Newfoundland, you will ensure a relaxed everyday life and you will benefit by achieving an intensive and intimate relationship with him. You will see, that people who ridicule your

methods, will be envious of your well-brought up dog.

Lastly, I have one more tip for you:

Read this book more than once. It would be best to read it several times before your Newfoundland moves in. While you are beginning your training, it will not harm to refer to this book from time to time.

I wish you and your puppy every imaginable success for your future. Above all, I wish you harmony, love and many years together.

Yours
Claudia

BOOK RECOMMENDATION FOR YOU

Get the second volume now and find out how to train your grown-up Newfoundland!

Newfoundland Training Vol 2– Dog Training for your grown-up Newfoundland

Dog training is often ...

- confused with classic basic training of puppies
- considered only suitable for particularly gifted dogs
- considered too difficult to achieve without experience
- replaced by anti-authoritarian methods.
- considered too difficult to achieve without experience.

What constitutes dog training and what is it good for? And how can you and your Newfoundland profit from it without having any experience?

Do you sometimes have the feeling that your dog has too much energy and does not feel fully stimulated, no matter how often you walk with him? Then dog training is the right thing for you. The simple but very effective methods of physical and mental training that you will read about in this guide will help you to stimulate your Newfoundland, in an appropriate way for his species, while at the same time having fun.

Get your copy of this book and discover...

- how to build up a unique relationship with your Newfoundland
- how you can stimulate him physically and mentally in an appropriate way for his species
- and all that without previous experience in this area.

Read about background information, read experience reports and obtain step-by-step instructions and secret tips which are tailor-made for your Newfoundland.

CLAUDIA KAISER
NEWFOUNDLAND
TRAINING VOL 3
Taking care of your Newfoundland
Nutrition, common diseases and general care of your Newfoundland
WITH
EXTRA CHAPTER:
RECIPIES
EXPERTEN
GRUPPE
VERLAG
GERMAN
QUALITY

Newfoundland Training Vol 3 - Taking care of your Newfoundland

Taking care of a dog is often ...

- underrated and regarded as being unnecessary.
- only related to the grooming of the fur.
- completely neglected by many owners.

What is really important about the care of your Newfoundland and how do you feed him properly? How can you recognise diseases and parasites early and, if possible, even prevent them?

If you want to know how and how often to check on your Newfoundland's eyes, ears, teeth, paws, fur and skin, this guidebook is exactly right for you. You will learn what to watch out for. You will also learn what to watch out for when you buy commercially prepared food and what the advantages and disadvantages are of the various alternative methods of feeding, such as home-cooked, BARF or vegetarian or vegan feeding. In addition, you will discover everything you need to know about vaccinations and castration to help you decide whether they are right for you and your Newfoundland.

Get your copy of this book and discover...

- How to feed your Newfoundland in a healthy way consistent with his breed.
- How to examine him to recognise disease early and to ensure his correct care.
- And all that without having any previous experience in that area.

Get the new mandala coloring book now with 55 wonderful dog motifs!

MANDALA COLORING BOOK DOGS - 55 animal motifs (dog theme) to colour-in for adults and children

Do you love colouring-in and are you very fond of dogs? Perhaps you are feeling very stressed at the moment and need a moment to relax, a time to switch-off and enjoy your own company?

You can do that with this book. Inside, 55 hand-picked motifs of dogs are waiting for you to bring them to life. Every picture is crafted with great care, creating a wonderful combination of animal drawing and mandalas.

While you are colouring-in, you will notice:

- how you can immerse yourself in the fantastic world of mandalas,
- how your body and mind come to rest and
- how you can leave stress behind you, through mindfulness and patience.

Immerse yourself in the world of mandalas and discover the 55 beautiful and individual dog mandalas contained in this colouring book. As if that is not enough, you will also receive additional 8 mandalas from the fantastic world of our colouring books – free!

Stimulate your imagination and enjoy a moment of peace and tranquillity, just for you!

DID YOU ENJOY MY BOOK?

Now you have read my book, you know how best to train your little Newfoundland puppy. This is why I am asking you now for a small favour. Customer reviews are an important part of every product offered by Amazon. It is the first thing that customers look at and, more often than not, is the main reason whether or not they decide to buy the product. Considering the endless number of products available at Amazon, this factor is becoming increasingly important.

If you liked my book, I would be more than grateful if you could leave your review by Amazon. How do you do that? Just click the "Write a customer review"-button (as shown below), which you find on the Amazon product page of my book or your orders site:

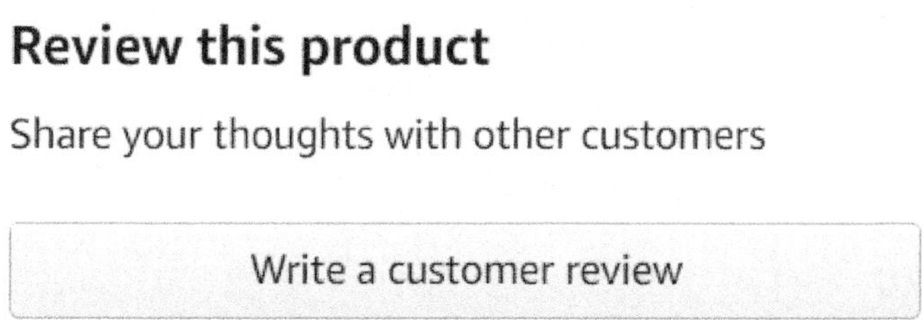

Just write a short review as to whether you particularly liked my book or if there is something I can improve on. It will not take more than 2 minutes, honestly!

Be assured, I will read every review personally. It will help me a lot to improve my books and to tailor them to your wishes.

For this I say to you:

Thank you very much!

Yours
Claudia

REFERENCES

Schlegl-Kofler, Katharina: Unser Welpe. 3rd edition. Munich: Published 2009 by GRÄFE UND UNZER

Schlegl-Kofler, Katharina: Hunde-erziehung. 3rd edition. Munich: Published 2009 by GRÄFE UND UNZER

Niewöhner, Imken: Auf ins Leben!: Grundschulplan für Welpen. 1st edition. Nerdlen: Published 2012 by Kynos

Rätke, Jana; Perfahl, Barbara: Abenteuer Welpe. 1st edition. Nerdlen: Published 2017 by Kynos

Millan, Cesar; Peltier, Melissa Jo: Tipps vom Hundeflüsterer: Einfache Maßnahmen für die gelungene Beziehung zwischen Mensch und Hund. 1st edition. Munich: Published 2009 by Arkana

Koring, Mel: Welpenschule: Das 8-Wochen-Training. 1st edition. Stuttgart: Published 2018 by Kosmos

Winkler, Sabine: So lernt mein Hund: Der Schlüssel für die erfolgreiche Erziehung und Ausbildung. 3rd edition. Stuttgart: Published by Kosmos

Neufundländer: d. Neufundländer u. Landseer-Neufundländer von Ippen, Heinrich 1985

Newfoundland Puppy Training Book for Newfoundland Puppies 2018 Karen Douglas Kane

Neufundländer und Landseer: Jubiläumsausgabe Taschenbuch 2006 Victor Goerttler

Neufundländer 2001 von Wulf A Gewert, Wolfgang Dettlaff

Neufundländer heute (Das besondere Hundebuch) 1999 von Hedd Richards, Del Richards

DISCLAIMER

1st Edition

 Publisher: GbR, Martin Seidel und Corinna Krupp, Bachstraße 37, 53498 Bad Breisig, Germany, email: info@expertengruppeverlag.de, Cover photo: www.depositphotos.com. The information provided within this book is for general information purposes only. It does not represent any recommendation or application of the methods mentioned within. The information in this book does not purport to imply or guarantee its completeness, accuracy, or topicality. This book in no way replaces the competent recommendations of, or care given by, a dog school. The author and publisher do not assume and hereby disclaims any liability for damages or disruption caused by the use of the information given herein.